# THE EYE-BEATERS,
# BLOOD, VICTORY,
# MADNESS, BUCKHEAD
## *and*
# MERCY

ALSO BY JAMES DICKEY

POETRY

*Into the Stone*

*Drowning with Others*

*Helmets*

*Two Poems of the Air*

*Buckdancer's Choice*

*Poems 1957-1967*

CRITICISM

*The Suspect in Poetry*

*Babel to Byzantium*

FICTION

*Deliverance*

# THE EYE-BEATERS, BLOOD, VICTORY, MADNESS, BUCKHEAD and MERCY

## James Dickey

HAMISH HAMILTON
LONDON

*To Lester Mansfield*

Poems in this book have previously been published as follows: Sugar, Under Buzzards, The Cancer Match, Venom, Blood and the last three sections of Pine in *Poetry*, Copyright © 1969 by Modern Poetry Association; Butterflies, Giving A Son To The Sea, The Place, The Lord In The Air, Knock, Madness and the first two sections of Pine appeared originally in *The New Yorker*; At Mercy Manor and Looking For The Buckhead Boys in *The Atlantic Monthly*, Copyright © 1969 by The Atlantic Monthly Company, and VICTORY in *The Atlantic Monthly*, Copyright © 1968 by The Atlantic Monthly Company; Turning Away in *Hudson Review*, Copyright © 1966 by The Hudson Review; The Eye-beaters and Living There in *Harper's Magazine*; For The First Manned Moon Orbit and The Ground in *Life*.

*First published in Great Britain, 1971*
*by Hamish Hamilton Ltd*
*90 Great Russell Street London W.C.1*

SBN 241 01965 6

*Printed in Great Britain by*
*Lowe & Brydone (Printers) Ltd., London*

# CONTENTS

# DIABETES

## I
### Sugar

One night I thirsted like a prince
Then like a king
Then like an empire     like a world
On fire. I rose and flowed away and fell
Once more to sleep. In an hour I was back
In the kingdom     staggering, my belly going round with self-
Made night-water, wondering what
The hell. Months of having a tongue
Of flame convinced me: I had better not go
On this way. The doctor was young

And nice. He said, I must tell you,
My friend, that it is needles moderation
And exercise. You don't want to look forward
To gangrene and kidney

Failure     boils blindness infection skin trouble falling
Teeth coma and death.
               O.K.
                      In sleep my mouth went dry
With my answer     and in it burned the sands
Of time with new fury. Sleep could give me no water
But my own. Gangrene in white
Was in my wife's hand at breakfast
Heaped like a mountain. Moderation, moderation,
My friend, and exercise. Each time the barbell
Rose     each time a foot fell
Jogging, it counted itself
One death     two death     three death and resurrection
For a little while. Not bad! I always knew it would have to be
                        somewhere around
The house: the real
Symbol of Time I could eat
And live with, coming true when I opened my mouth:

True in the coffee and the child's birthday
Cake     helping sickness be fire-
tongued, sleepless and water-
logged     but not bad, sweet sand
Of time, my friend, an everyday—
A livable death at last.


## II
*Under Buzzards*

[for Robert Penn Warren]


Heavy summer. Heavy. Companion, if we climb our mortal bodies
High with great effort, we shall find ourselves
Flying with the life
Of the birds of death. We have come up
Under buzzards     they face us

Slowly     slowly circling     and as we watch them they turn us
Around, and you and I spin
Slowly, slowly rounding
Out the hill. We are level
Exactly on this moment: exactly on the same bird-

plane with those deaths. They are the salvation of our sense
Of glorious movement. Brother, it is right for us to face
Them every which way, and come to ourselves and come
From every direction
There is. Whirl and stand fast!
Whence cometh death, O Lord?
On the downwind, riding fire,

Of Hogback Ridge.
               But listen: what is dead here?
They are not falling but waiting     but waiting
Riding, and they may know
The rotten, nervous sweetness of my blood.
Somewhere riding the updraft
Of a far forest fire, they sensed the city sugar
The doctors found in time.
My eyes are green as lettuce with my diet,
My weight is down,

One pocket nailed with needles and injections, the other dragging
        With sugar cubes to balance me in life
                And hold my blood
Level, level. Tell me, black riders, does this do any good?
        Tell me what I need to know about my time
                In the world. O out of the fiery


Furnace of pine-woods, in the sap-smoke and crownfire of needles,
        Say when I'll die. When will the sugar rise boiling
                Against me, and my brain be sweetened
                to death?
                        *In heavy summer, like this day.*
        All right! Physicians, witness! I will shoot my veins
                Full of insulin. Let the needle burn
                In. From your terrible heads
        The flight-blood drains        and you are falling back
                Back to the body-raising


        Fire.
                Heavy summer. Heavy. My blood is clear
        For a time. Is it too clear? Heat waves are rising
        Without birds. But something is gone from me,
        Friend. This is too sensible. Really it is better
        To know when to die        better for my blood
                To stream with the death-wish of birds.
                You know, I had just as soon crush
                        This doomed syringe
Between two mountain rocks, and bury this needle in needles


        Of trees. Companion, open that beer.
                How the body works        how hard it works
                        For its medical books is not
                        Everything: everything is how
                Much glory is in it: heavy summer is right


        For a long drink of beer. Red sugar of my eyeballs
                        Feels them turn blindly
                In the fire        rising        turning        turning
                Back to Hogback Ridge, and it is all
Delicious, brother: my body is turning        is flashing unbalanced
        Sweetness everywhere, and I am calling my birds.

# MESSAGES

[to and from my sons]

## I
### *Butterflies*

Over and around     grass banked and packed short and holding back
Water, we have been
Playing, my son, in pure abandon,
And we still are. We play, and play inside our play and play
Inside of that, where butterflies are increasing
The deeper we get
And lake-water ceases to strain. Ah, to play in a great field of light
With your son, both men, both
Young and old! Ah, it was then, Chris,

As now! You lay down on the earth
Dam, and I rambled forth and did not look and found
And found like a blueprint of animal
Life, the whole skeleton of a cow. O son, left
In pure abandon, I sat down inside the bones in the light
Of pine trees, studying the tiny holes
In the head, and where the ants
Could not get through, the nerves had left
Their messages. I sat in the unmoving hearse
Flying, carried by cow-bones in pure
Abandon, back to you. I picked up the head
And inside the nose-place were packets
And whole undealt decks
Of thin bones, like shaved playing cards.
I won the horns. They twisted loose from the forehead
And would not twist back     as I gambled and rocked
With the skull in my lap,
The cow not straining to live. In that car I rode
Far off
     and in
          and in
While you were sleeping off the light
Of the world.
          And when I came

From the bone dust in pure abandon, I found you lying on the earth
Dam, slanted in the grass that held back
The water, your hands behind your head,
Gazing through your eyelids into the universal
Light, and the butterflies were going

  . . . Here


                                            here


              here
              here


                                        from here


    madly over


                          to


     here


                                        here.


They went over you     here     and through you
Here    no    yes and tattered apart,
Beat out over water and back
To earth, and over my oldest
Son asleep: their ragged, brave wings
Pulsed on the blue flowers    shook like the inmost
Play    and blazed all over and around
Where you slept holding back
Water without strain.
              That is all, but like all joy

On earth and water,
in bones and in wings and in light,
It is a gamble. It is play, son, now
As then. I put the horns beside you in the grass
And turned back to my handsprings and my leaps.


## II
### *Giving a Son to the Sea*

Gentle blondness and the moray eel go at the same time
On in my mind as you grow, who fired at me at the age
Of six, a Christmas toy for child
Spies: a bullet with a Special Secret
Message Compartment. My hands undid the bullet meant
For my heart, and it read aloud
"I love you." That message hits me most
When I watch you swim, that being your only talent.
The sea obsesses you, and your room is full of it:

Your room is full
of flippers and snorkels and books
On spearfishing.
O the depths,
My gentle son. Out of that room and into the real
Wonder and weightless horror
Of water      into the shifts of vastness
You will probably go, for someone must lead
Mankind, your father and your sons,
Down there to live, or we all die
Of crowding. Many of yóu
Will die, in the cold roll
Of the bottom currents, and the life lost
More totally than anywhere, there in the dark
Of no breath at all.
And I must let you go, out of your gentle
Childhood into your own man suspended
In its body, slowly waving its feet
Deeper and deeper, while the dark grows, the cold
Grows careless, the sun is put
Out by the weight of the planet
As it sinks to the bottom. Maybe you will find us there

An agonizing new life, much like the life
Of the drowned, where we will farm eat sleep and bear children
Who dream of birds.
                    Switch on your sea-lamp, then,
And go downward, son, with your only message
Echoing. Your message to the world, remember,
          Came to your father
At Christmas like a bullet. When the great fish roll
With you, herded deep in the deepest dance,
When the shark cuts through your invisible
          Trail, I will send back
That message, though nothing that lives
Underwater will ever receive it.
That does not matter, my gentle blond
          Son. That does not matter.

# MERCY

Ah, this night      this night mortality wails out
Over Saint Joseph's      this night and every      over Mercy      Mercy
Mercy Manor. Who can be dressed right for the long cry
Who can have his tie knotted to suit the cinder Doctors'
Parking Lot? O yes I'm walking      and we go      I go
In      into a whorehouse
And convent rolled
Into      into something      into the slant streets of slum
Atlanta. I've brought the House Mother
A bottle of gin. She goes for ice
Rattling the kitchen somewhere over      under
The long cry. Fay hasn't come in
Yet; she's scrubbing
For Doctor Evans. Television bulks as the girls pass
In, rising
Up the stairs, and one says to me, What
Say, Good Looking. Something wails like a held-down saint
In Saint Joseph's. The kids, the Mother      the House
Mother says, all act like babies these days. Some of them are, I say
In a low scream. Not all, she says, not all.
You ever been a nurse?
I ask. No; my husband was in wholesale furniture.
Passed away last year of a kidney
Disease; they couldn't do anything for him
At all: he said you go and work
With those girls who've been so good
To me. And here I am, Good
Looking. Fay ought to be
Here in a little while.
The girls that went up are coming
Down, turning the leaves
Of the sign-out book. You waiting for Fay? Yes.
She'll be a little while. O.K.

More ice, to ice-pack
The gin. The last door opens.
It is Fay. This night mortality wails out. Who died,
My love? Whom could you not do anything for? Is that some stranger's
Blood on your thigh? O love I know you by the lysol smell you give
Vaseline. Died      died
On the table.
She'll just be a minute. These are good girls, the Mother
Says. Fay's a good girl. She's been married; her aunt's
Keeping the kids. I reckon you know that, though. I do,
And I say outside
Of time, there must be some way she can strip
Blood off      somebody's blood      strip and comb down and out
That long dark hair. She's overhead
Naked she's streaming
In the long cry      she has her face in her hands
In the shower, thinking of children
Her children in and out
Of Saint Joseph's      she is drying      my eyes burn
Like a towel      and perfume and disinfectant battle
In her armpits      she is stamping
On the ceiling to get her shoes to fit: Lord, Lord, where are you,
Fay? O yes, you big cow-bodied
Love o yes you have changed
To black      you are in deep
Dark and your pale face rages
With fatigue. Mother      Mother      House
Mother of Mercy
Manor, you can have the rest
Of the gin. The cinders of the parking lot are blazing all around
Saint Joseph's; the doctors are leaving. Turn out the light as you go up
To your husband's furniture, and come
Here to me, you big
Bosomed hard handed hard
Working worker for Life, you. I'll give you something
Good      something like a long cry
Out over the ashes of cars      something like a scream through
hundreds of bright
Bolted-down windows. O take me into
Your black. Without caring, care
For me. Hold my head in your wide scrubbed

(15)

                    Hands bring up
                  My lips. I wail like all
              Saint Joseph's    like mortality
              This night     and I nearly am dead
        In love     Collapsed on the street     struck down
                  By my heart, with the wail
              Coming to me, borne in ambulances voice
            By voice into Saint Joseph's     nearly dead
              On arrival     on the table beyond
                  All help: She would bend
                Over me like this     sink down
                  With me in her white dress
                Changing to black     we sink
                      Down flickering
            Like television     like Arthur Godfrey's face
              Coming on     huge     happy
                  About us     happy
              About everything     O bring up
          My lips     hold them down don't let them cry
        With the cry     close     closer     eyeball to eyeball
                In my arms, O queen of death
                Alive, and with me at the end.

# TWO POEMS OF GOING HOME

## I
### *Living There*

                    The Keeper
        Is silent      is living in the air not
          Breathable, of time. It is gray
          Winter in the woods where he lives.
        They've been cut down; you can see through
        What he is keeping      what used to be a room
            In a house with one side turned
        To trees. There are no woods now, only other
Houses. Old Self like a younger brother, like a son, we'd come rambling
        Out of the house in wagons, turn off the back
        Driveway and bump at full bump-speed down
          Through the woods, the branches flickering
            With us, with the whole thing of home
    A blur, gone rolling in leaves. But people are always coming

        To know woods      to know rooms in houses
      That've been torn down. Where we live, you and I,
              My youth and my middle
        Age      where we live with our family, miles away
            From home, from my old home,
                  I have rooms
      I keep, but these old one, the ones where I grew
              Up, are in the air
              Of winter they are over
      Other houses like ghosts. The house lives only
          In my head while I look and the sun sinks
        Through the floors that were here: the floors
      Of time. Brother, it is a long way to the real

        House I keep. Those rooms are growing
            Intolerable in minds I made
        Up, though all seems calm when I walk
Into them as though I belonged there. Sleepers are stirring      an arm lies
          Over a face, and the lights are burning

In the fish tank. It is not like this,
But it will be. One day those forms will rise
And leave      and age
And come back      and that house will flame like this
In the Keeper's head
With the last sun; it will be gone,
And someone will not be able
To believe there is only nothing

Where his room was, next to his father's
Blue-eyed      blue-eyed      the fixer      the wagon-master
Blazing in death
With life: will not be able to look
Into windows of the room where he saw,
For the first time, his own blood.
That room fills only with dying
Solar flame      with only the backyard wind
Only the lack
Of trees, of the screech-owl my mother always thought
Was a hurt dog. And tell me for the Lord God
's sake, where are all our old
Dogs?
Home?
Which way is that?
Is it this vacant lot? These woven fences?
Or is it hundreds

Of miles away, where I am the Keeper
Of rooms turning night and day
Into memory? Is it the place I now live
And die in      the place I manage
In? Is it with those people who never knew
*These* people, except for me? Those people sleeping
Eating my food      loading
Their minds with love      their rooms with what they love
And must lose, and cannot forget? Those fish
Tanks      those James Bond posters      those telescopes
And microscopes and the hidden pictures
Of naked girls? Who are they? And will they come foolishly
Back to stare at nothing
But sunset, where the blood flowed and the wagon wheel grew whole in the
hands

(18)

Of the bald-headed father? Will they look into those rooms where now
They sleep, and see nothing but moonlight      nothing but everything
                    Far and long
        Gone, long gone? Why does the Keeper go blind
      With sunset? The mad, weeping Keeper who can't keep
    A God-damned thing      who knows he can't keep everything
        Or anything alive: none of his rooms, his people
                His past, his youth, himself,
            But cannot let them die? Yes, I keep
Some of those people, not in wagons but in the all-night glimmer
            Of fish      in the secret glimmer
            Of unfolding girls. I think I know—
    I know them well. I call them, for a little while, sons.

## II
*Looking for the Buckhead Boys*

Some of the time, going home, I go
Blind and can't find it.
The house I lived in growing up and out
The doors of high school is torn
Down and cleared
Away for further development, but that does not stop me.
First in the heart
Of my blind spot are
The Buckhead Boys. If I can find them, even one,
I'm home. And if I can find him      catch him in or around
Buckhead, I'll never die: it's likely my youth will walk
Inside me like a king.

First of all, going home, I must go
To Wender and Roberts' Drug Store, for driving through I saw it
Shining      renewed      renewed
In chromium, but still there.
It's one of the places the Buckhead Boys used to be, before
Beer turned teen-ager.
                    Tommy Nichols
Is not there. The Drug Store is full of women
Made of cosmetics. Tommy Nichols has never been
In such a place: he was the Number Two Man on the Mile
Relay Team in his day.
                    What day?
My day. Where was I?
                    Number Three, and there are some sunlit pictures
In the Book of the Dead to prove it: the 1939
North Fulton High School Annual. Go down,
Go down

To Tyree's Pool Hall, for there was more
Concentration of the spirit
Of the Buckhead Boys
In there, than anywhere else in the world.
                              Do I want some shoes
To walk all over Buckhead like a king

(20)

Nobody knows? Well, I can get them at Tyree's;
It's a shoe store now. I could tell you where every spittoon
Ought to be standing. Charlie Gates used to say one of these days
I'm gonna get myself the reputation of being
The bravest man in Buckhead. I'm going in Tyree's toilet
And pull down my pants and take a shit.
                                                        Maybe
Charlie's the key: the man who would say that would never leave
Buckhead. Where is he? Maybe I ought to look up
Some Old Merchants. Why didn't I think of that
        Before?
                        Lord, Lord! Like a king!


Hardware. Hardware and Hardware Merchants
        Never die, and they have everything on hand
There is to know. Somewhere in the wood-screws Mr. Hamby may have
        My Prodigal's Crown on sale. He showed up
                For every football game at home
Or away, in the hills of North Georgia. There he is, as old
As ever.
                Mr. Hamby, remember me?
                                        God A'Mighty! Ain't you the one
Who fumbled the punt and lost the Russell game?
                                                        That's right.
                How're them butter fingers?
                                        Still butter, I say,
Still fumbling. But what about the rest of the team? What about Charlie
        Gates?
                He the boy that got lime in his eye from the goal line
When y'all played Gainesville?
                                        Right.
                                I don't know. Seems to me I see . . .


*See? See? What does Charlie Gates see in his eye burning*
*With the goal line? Does he see a middle-aged man from the Book*
        *Of the Dead looking for him in magic shoes*
*From Tyree's disappeared pool hall?*
                                        Mr. Hamby, Mr. Hamby,
Where? Where is Mont Black?
                                        Paralyzed. Doctors can't do nothing.
                Where is Dick Shea?
                                        Assistant Sales Manager

Of Kraft Cheese.
How about Punchy Henderson?
Died of a heart attack
Watching high school football
In South Carolina.
*Old Punchy, the last*
*Of the windsprinters, and now for no reason the first*
*Of the heart attacks.*
Harmon Quigley?
He's up at County Work Farm
Sixteen. Doing all right up there; be out next year.

Didn't anybody get to be a doctor
Or lawyer?
Sure. Bobby Laster's a chiropractor. He's right out here
At Bolton; got a real good business.
Jack Siple?
Moved away.
Gordon Hamm?
Dead
In the war.

*O the Book*
*Of the Dead, and the dead bright sun on the page*
*Where the team stands ready to explode*
*In all directions with Time.* Did you say you see Charlie
Gates every now and then?
Seems to me.
Where?
He may be out yonder at the Gulf Station between here and Sandy
Springs.

Let me go pull my car out
Of the parking lot in back
Of Wender and Roberts'. Do I need gas? No; let me drive around the block
Let me drive around Buckhead
A few dozen times      turning      turning in my foreign
Car till the town spins      whirls till the chrome vanishes
From Wender and Roberts'      the spittoons are remade
From the sun itself      the dead pages flutter the hearts rise up, that lie
In the ground, and Bobby Laster's backbreaking fingers
Pick up a cue-stick      Tommy Nichols and I rack the balls

(22)

And Charlie Gates walks into Tyree's un-
imaginable toilet.
I go north
Now, and I can use fifty
Cents' worth of gas.
It is Gulf. I pull in and praise the Lord Charlie
Gates comes out. His blue shirt dazzles
Like a baton-pass. He squints he looks at me
Through the goal line. Charlie, Charlie, we have won away from
We have won at home
In the last minute. Can you see me? You say
What I say: where in God
Almighty have you been all this time? I don't know,
Charlie. I don't know. But I've come to tell you a secret
That has to be put into code. Understand what I mean when I say
To the one man who came back alive
From the Book of the Dead        to the bravest man
In Buckhead        to the lime-eyed ghost
Blue-wavering in the fumes
Of good Gulf gas, "Fill 'er up."
With wine? Light? Heart-attack blood? The contents of Tyree's toilet?
The beer
Of teen-age sons? No; just
"Fill 'er up. Fill 'er up, Charlie."

# THE PLACE

We are nerve-blowing now. Unspeaking and whiteness around. Warm wind
Was never here. Snow has no move. So this
Has placed us. Dark is with it nearly, for this last of day-
Shaking of shores.

Night is down on us; hold me with all your fur.
These waters have put every grain of their ice
Into our red hand-marrow. Statue-faced, let us breathe
On each other      let us breathe the ice

Sweeping into the air, for it has crossed to
Within us, rigidly airborne, impassable from crossing
Miles of lake-freeze in our
Overwhelming direction. They hang true lovers with thread-

steel through the nose. It hurts straight up and down
Inside us. This is where we come, and we are cross-
eyed with love and every tooth
root aches. Lover, this is where:

I can tell you here.

# APOLLO

. . . whoever lives out there in space must surely
call Earth "the blue planet" . . .

ED WHITE

## I. *For the First Manned Moon Orbit*

So long
So long as the void
Is hysterical, bolted out, you float on nothing

But procedure alone,

Eating, sleeping like a man
Deprived of the weight of his own
And all humanity in the name

Of a new life
and through this, making new
Time slowly, the moon comes.
Its mountains bulge
They crack they hold together
Closer     spreading     smashed crust
Of uncanny rock     ash-glowing     alchemicalizing the sun
With peace: with the peace of a country
Bombed-out by the universe.
You lean back from the great light-
shattered face     the pale blaze
Of God-stone coming

Close     too close, and the dead seas turn
The craters hover     turn
Their dark side to kill
The radio, and the one voice
Of earth.
You and your computers have brought out
The silence of mountains the animal
Eye has not seen since the earth split,
Since God first found geometry
Would move     move
In mysterious ways. You hang

Mysteriously, pulling     the moon-dark pulling,
And solitude breaks down
Like an electrical system: it is something

Else: nothing is something
Something I am trying

(26)

To say O God
Almighty! To come back! To complete the curve       to come back
Singing with procedure       back through the last dark
Of the moon, past the dim ritual
Random stones of oblivion, and through the blinding edge
Of moonlight into the sun

And behold

The blue planet steeped in its dream

Of reality, its calculated vision shaking with
The only love.


## II. *The Moon Ground*

. You look as though
You know me, though the world we came from is striking
You in the forehead like Apollo. Buddy,
We have brought the gods. We know what it is to shine
Far off, with earth. We alone
Of all men, could take off
Our shoes and fly. One-sixth of ourselves, we have gathered,
Both of us, under another one
Of us overhead. He is reading the dials he is understanding
Time, to save our lives. You and I are in earth
light and deep moon
shadow on magic ground
Of the dead new world, and we do not but we could
Leap over each other like children in the universal playground
Of stones
but we must not play
At being here: we must look
We must look for it: the stones are going to tell us
Not the why but the how of all things. Brother, your gold face flashes
On me. It is the earth. I hear your deep voice rumbling from the body
Of its huge clothes       Why did we come here
It does not say, but the ground looms, and the secret
Of time is lying

Within amazing reach. It is everywhere
We walk, our glass heads shimmering with absolute heat
And cold. We leap slowly
Along it. We will take back the very stones
Of Time, and build it where we live. Or in the cloud
striped blue of home, will the secret crumble
In our hands with air? Will the moon-plague kill our children
In their beds? The Human Planet trembles in its black
Sky with what we do     I can see it hanging in the god-gold only
Brother of your face. We are this world: we are
The only men. What hope is there at home
In the azure of breath, or here with the stone
Dead secret? My massive clothes bubble around me
Crackling with static and Gray's
Elegy helplessly coming
From my heart, and I say I think something
From high school I remember Now
Fades the glimmering landscape on the sight, and all the air
A solemn stillness holds. Earth glimmers
And in its air-color a solemn stillness holds
It. O brother! Earth-faced god! APOLLO! My eyes blind
With unreachable tears     my breath goes all over
Me and cannot escape. We are here to do one
Thing only, and that is rock by rock to carry the moon to take it
Back. Our clothes embrace we cannot touch we cannot
Kneel. We stare into the moon
dust, the earth-blazing ground. We laugh, with the beautiful craze
Of static. We bend, we pick up stones.

# THE CANCER MATCH

Lord, you've sent both
And may have come yourself. I will sit down, bearing up under
The death of light very well, and we will all
Have a drink. Two or three, maybe.
I see now the delights

Of being let "come home"
From the hospital.
Night!
I don't have all the time
In the world, but I have all night.
I have space for me and my house,
And I have cancer and whiskey

In a lovely relation.
They are squared off, here on my ground. They are fighting,
Or are they dancing? I have been told     and told
That medicine has no hope, or anything
More to give,

But they have no idea
What hope is, or how it comes. You take these two things:
This bourbon and this thing growing. Why,
They are like boys! They bow
To each other

Like judo masters,
One of them jumping for joy, and I watch them struggle
All around the room, inside and out
Of the house, as they battle
Near the mailbox

And superbly
For the street-lights! Internally, I rise like my old self
To watch: and remember, ladies and gentlemen,

We are looking at this match
From the standpoint

Of tonight
Alone. Swarm over him, my joy, my laughter, my Basic Life
Force! Let your bright sword-arm stream
Into that turgid hulk, the worst
Of me, growing:

Get 'im, O Self
Like a beloved son! One more time! Tonight we are going
Good      better and better      we are going
To win, and not only win but win
Big, win big.

# VENOM

[for William Haast]

Forever, it comes from the head. *Where does it end?*
In life-blood. All over it, in fact, like thrown
Off and thrown-again light. There is little help
For it, but there is some.

*The priest of poison: where is he? Who is*
*His latest snake? How does he work?*

He has taken it all, brother, and his body lies
With its hand in ice, in a lung

Of iron
                    but at last he rises, his heart changing
What the snake thought. Tooth-marks all over
Him are chattering of life, not death, not
What God gave them. He shimmers

With healing. He will lie down again
With him the snake has entered.
His blood will flow the length
Of the veins of both. They will clasp arms and double-dream

Of the snake in the low long smothering
Sun. Look down! They stretch out giving
And taking. Clouds of family beat the windows
Of doctors with their breath. Here lies

The man made good by a hundred
Bites. It is not God but a human
Body they pray to: Turn the poison
Round turn it back on itself O turn it

Good: better than life they whisper:
Turn it, they hammer whitely:
                    Turn it, turn it,
                    Brother.

# BLOOD

In a cold night
Of somebody. Is there other
Breath? What did I say?
Or do?

Mercy.
MERCY!

There is nothing,
But did I do it? I did something.
Merciful, merciful
O God, what? And

Am I still drunk?
Not enough O

Is there any light O where
Do you *touch* this room?
O father

Of Heaven my head cannot
Lift but my hand maybe—
Nobody is breathing      what weapon
Was it? Light smashes

Down there is nothing but
Blood blood all over

Me and blood. Her hair is smeared.
My God what has got loose
In here at last? Who *is*

This girl? She is
Some other town some far
From home: knife

Razor, fingernails O she has been opened
Somewhere and yet

She sighs she turns in the slaughtered sheets
To me in the blood of her children.
Where in what month?

In the cold in the blood
Of life, she turns
to me, and my weapon
will never recover its blood.
Who is

This woman? No matter; she is safe.
She is safe with me.

# IN THE POCKET

NFL

Going backward
All of me and some
Of my friends are forming a shell     my arm is looking
Everywhere and some are breaking
In      breaking down
And out   breaking
Across, and one is going deep      deeper
Than my arm. Where is Number One hooking
Into the violent green alive
With linebackers? I cannot find him he cannot beat
His man      I fall back more
Into the pocket      it is raging and breaking
Number Two has disappeared into the chalk
Of the sideline      Number Three is cutting with half
A step of grace      my friends are crumbling
Around me the wrong color
Is looming      hands are coming
Up and over between
My arm and Number Three: throw it hit him in the middle
Of his enemies      hit move scramble
Before death and the ground
Come up  LEAP STAND KILL DIE STRIKE

Now.

# KNOCK

Sharing    what sharing    quickly who
Is outside    in    both you together here
And unseen out    let the bed huddle and jump

Naked in the quick dead middle
Of the night, making what is to be
There    you being broken by something

Open where the door thins out
Making frames of the room's early-
warning wood    is the code still

The same can the five fingers
Of the hand still show against
Anything? Have they come for us?

# VICTORY

By September 3rd I had made my bundle
Of boards and a bag of nails. America, I was high
On Okinawa, with the fleet lying on its back
Under me, whispering "I can't help it"

                and all ships firing up fire
Fighting liquids     sucking seawater, hoses climbing and coloring
The air, for Victory. I was clear-seeing
The morning    far-seeing backward
And forward from the cliff. I turned on the ground
And dug in, my nails and bag of magic
Boards from the tent-floor trembling to be
A throne. I was ready to sail
The island toward life
After death, left hand following right into the snail
shelled ground, then knocking down and nailing down my chair like a box
seat in the worldwide window of peace    and sat and lay down my arms
On the stomped grains of ammo-crates heavy with the soles
Of buddies who had helped me wreck the tent
In peace-joy, and of others long buried
At sea. The island rocked with the spectrum
Bombardment of the fleet    and there I was
For sure    saved and plucked naked to my shirt
And lids. I raised my head to the sun.
What I saw was two birthdays

Back, in the jungle, before I sailed high on the rainbow
Waters of victory    before the sun
Of armistice morning burned into my chest
The great V of Allied Conquest. Now it was not here
With the ships sucking up fire
Water and spraying it wild
Through every color, or where, unthreatened, my navel burned
Burned like an entry-wound. Lord, I deepened
Memory, and lay in the light high and wide
Open, murmuring "I can't help it" as I went

South in my mind.

                                        Yes Mother

                    there were two fine hands
Driving the jeep: mine, much better than before, for you had sent
Whiskey. What could I do but make the graveyards soar! O you coming
        Allied Victory, I rambled in the night of two birthdays
                Ago, the battle of Buna stoned
        In moonlight      stone-dead left and right      going nowhere
            Near friend or foe, but turned off into the thickest
    Dark. O yes, Mother, let me tell you: the vines split and locked:
                About where you'd never know me is
                Where I stalled
                                    and sat bolt up-
                    right in the moonlit bucket
        Seat throne of war
                                    cascading the bottle to drink
        To victory, and to what I would do, when the time came,
            With my body. The world leapt like the world
Driving nails, and the moon burned with the light it had when it split

                From the earth. I slept and it was foretold
                That I would live. My head came true
    In a great smile. I reached for the bottle. It was dying and the moon
                Writhed closer to be free; it could answer
    My smile of foreknowledge. I forgot the mosquitoes that were going
            Mad on my blood, of biting me once too often on the bites
        Of bites. Had the Form in the moon come from the dead soldier
            Of your bottle, Mother? Let down in blocked
        Out light, a snakehead hung, its eyes putting into mine
Visions of a victory at sea. New Guinea froze. Midair was steady

                Between. Snake-eyes needle-eyed      its
                    Lips halving its head
                Stayed shut. I held up the last drop
                In the bottle, and invited him
                    To sin      to celebrate
        The Allied victory to come. He pulled back a little over
                The evil of the thing I meant
    To stand for brotherhood. Nightshining his scales on Detroit
                Glass, he stayed on and on
                My mind. I found out the angel

                            (39)

Of peace is limbless and the day will come
I said, when no difference is between
My skin and the great fleets
Delirious with survival. Mother, I was drunk enough on your birthday
Present, not to die there. I backed the jeep out
Of the Buna weeds
                              and, finally, where the sun struck
The side of the hill, there I was
                                          back from the dark side
Of the mind, burning like a prism over the conquering Catherine
Wheel of the fleet. But ah, I turned

                    I sank I lay back dead
    Drunk on a cold table       I had closed my eyes
        And gone north       and lay to change
Colors all night. Out of the Nothing of occupation
Duty, I must have asked for the snake: I asked or the enemy told
                    Or my snakeskin told
Itself to be. Before I knew it in Yokahama, it was at my throat
    Beginning with its tail, cutting through the world
            wide Victory sign       moving under
            My armpit like a sailor's, scale
By scale. Carbon-arc-light spat in the faces of the four
Men who bent over me, for the future lay brilliantly in
The needles of the enemy. Naked I lay on their zinc
        Table, murmuring "I can't help it."
        He coiled around me, yet

        Headless       I turned with him side
            To side, as the peaceful enemy
        Designed       a spectrum of scales O yes
Mother I was in the tattoo parlor to this day
Not knowing how I got there as he grew,
        Red scales sucking up color       blue
White with my skin running out of the world
Wide sun. Frothing with pinpricks, filling with ink
            I lay and it lay
Now over my heart       limbless I fell and moved like moonlight
    On the needles       moving to hang my head
In a drunk boy's face, and watch him while he dreamed
        Of victory at sea. I retched but choked
It back, for he had crossed my breast, and I knew that many-

colored snakeskin was living with my heart     our hearts
Beat as one     port-of-call red     Yokahoma blue
O yes and now he lay low


On my belly, and gathered together the rainbow
Ships of Buckner Bay. I slumbered deep and he crossed the small
Of my back     increased
His patchwork hold on my hip     passed through the V between
My legs, and came
Around once more     all but the head     then I was turning     the snake
Coiled round my right thigh and crossed
Me with light hands     I felt myself opened
Just enough, where the serpent staggered on his last
Colors     needles gasping for air     jack-hammering
My right haunch burned by the hundreds
Of holes, as the snake shone on me complete     escaping
Forever     surviving     crushing     going home
To the bowels of the living,
His master, and the new prince of peace.

# THE LORD IN THE AIR

. . . If the spectator could . . . make a
friend & companion of one of these Images
of wonder . . . then would he meet the Lord
in the air & . . . be happy.     BLAKE

Shook down      shook up on these trees they have come
From moment to this moment floating on      in      and this
Moment changes now not with the light for my son
Has come      has come out with one crow floating
Off a limb      back on and off      off a limb in other
Sunlight turning and making him call himself

Blacker      then settles back      back into the other
Moment. They hunch and face in. O yes they are all in
These very trees of the son-faced and fenced-
in backyard      waiting for my boy and the Lord
In the air. O parents great things can be released
From your left-handed son's left hand! They don't know

It, but he has them all in his palm, and now puts them
All in his mouth. Out by the blue swoon of the pool
He lifts the wood whistle to his blond lips. A scratch-
long sound rises out of him      the trees flap and fall
Back, and ah there are crows dealt out all over inside
The light      they mix and mingle      dive      swerve throughout

Themselves      calling      self-shuffling      saying
With my boy's other tongue      sailing      meeting the Lord
Of their stolen voice in the air      and more incoming from miles
Away are here      they wheel in blast after blast
In the child's lungs, as he speaks to them in the only
Word they understand      the *one*      the syllable that means

Everything to them      he has them cold: their several
Accents      they cry with him they know more than all
They have known      fear grief good danger love and marriage

With the Lord in the air. The pool trembles     my boy falls
From his voice     falls in stitches to the concrete     one
More word he says     not intended     never heard     he gives

Them a tone never struck in the egg     in the million years
Of their voice     the whole sky laughs with crows     they creak
And croak with hilarity     black winged belly-laughs they tell
Each other     the great joke of flight     sound living
Deep in the sun and waiting     a sound more or less     or more
Like warning, like marriage. O Chris come in, drop off now

Black birds from your tongue of wood, back into our neighbor
Trees     into other dimensions, their added-to moment and light
Plays over the pool in lovely silence like new     surely like new
Power over birds and beasts: something that has come in
From all over     come out but not for betrayal, or to call
Up death or desire, but only to give     give what was never.

# PINE

successive apprehensions

## I

Low-cloudly it whistles, changing heads
On you. How hard to hold and shape head-round.
So any hard hold
Now loses; form breathes near. Close to forest-form
By ear, so landscape is eyelessly
Sighing through needle-eyes. O drawn off
The deep end, step right up
And be where. It could be a net
Spreading field: mid-whistling crossed with an edge and a life
Guarding sound. Overhead assign the bright and dark
Heels distance-running from all     overdrawing the only sound
Of this sound    sound of a life-mass
Drawn in long lines in the air    unbroken    brother-saving
Sound merely soft
And loudly soft just in time    then nothing and then
Soft    soft and a little caring-for    sift-softening
And soared-to. O ankle-wings lightening and fleeing
Brothers sending back for you
To join the air and live right: O justice-scales leaning toward mercy
Wherever. Justice is exciting in the wind
As escape continuing    as an ax hurling
Toward sound and shock. Nothing so just as wind
In its place in low cloud
Of its tree-voice stopped and on-going    footless flight
Sound like brothers coming on as
All-comers coming and fleeing
From ear-you and pine, and all pine.

## II

What mainly for the brow-hair
Has been blowing, dimensions and glows in:

Air the most like
Transfusion expands and only
There it is fresh
From overhead, steep-brewing and heavy from deep
Down upcoming new
To the lungs like a lean cave swimming—
Throat-light and iron
Warm spray on the inside face
Cutting often and cooling-out and brow
Opening and haunting freshly. So have you changed to this
You like a sea-wall
Tarred as a stump and blowing
Your skull like clover     lung-swimming in rosin
Dwelling
by breath
breath:
Whose head like a cave opens living
With eddies   needle-sapped out
Of its mind by this face-lifting
Face like a tree-beast
Listening, resetting the man-broken nose
bones on wine
Currents, as taste goes wild
And wells up   recalls   recovers and calls
For its own, for pure spirit
Food: windfalls and wavers out again.
From nothing, in green sinus-packs.


### III


More and more, through slow breaks
In the wind   no a different no this
Wind, another life of you rises,
A saliva-gland burns like a tree.
You are what you eat
and what will flutter
Like food if you turn completely
To your mouth, and stand wide open?
A wafer of bark, another
Needle, bitter rain by the mouthful coming.

Hunger swirls and slowly down
Showers      and are your children
What you eat? What green of horror
And manna in the next eye
To come from you? And will he whistle
From head to foot?

Bitter rain by the mouthful coming.


## IV

More hands on the terrible rough.
More pain but more than all
Is lodged in the leg-insides. More holding,
Though, more swaying. Rise and ride
Like this and wear and ride
Away with a passionate faceful
Of ply and points. The whole thing turns
On earth, throwing off a dark
Flood of four ways
Of being here blind and bending
Blacked-out and framed
Suspended and found alive in the rough palm-
And thigh-fires of friction, embracing in the beyond
It all, where,
Opening one by one, you still can open
One thing more. A final form
And color at last comes out
Of you alone putting it all
Together like nothing
Here like almighty


## V

Glory.

# MADNESS

(Time: Spring. Place: Virginia. A
domestic dog wanders from the house,
is bitten by a rabid female fox, runs
mad himself, and has to be hunted
down, killed, and beheaded.)

Lay in the house mostly living
With children when they called     mostly
Under the table begging for scraps lay with the head
On a family foot
Or stretched out on a side,
Firesided. Had no running
Running, ever.
Would lie relaxed, eyes dim

With appreciation, licking the pure contentment
Of long     long notched
Black lips. Would lap up milk like a cat and swim clear
In brown grateful eyes. That was then, before the Spring
Lay down and out
Under a tree, not far but a little far and out
Of sight of the house.
Rain had sown thick and gone

From the house where the living
Was done, where scraps fell and fire banked full
On one sleeping side of the spirit
Of the household
                    and it was best
To get up and wander
Out, out of sight. Help me was shouted
To the world of females     anyone will do
To the smoking leaves.

Love could be smelt. All things burned deep
In eyes that were dim from looking
At the undersides of tables     patient with being the god
Of small children. In Spring it is better with no

(47)

Doors which the god
Of households must beg at   no locks where the wind blows
The world's furry women
About in heat. And there

She lay, firesided, bushy-assed, her head
On the ground wide open, slopping soap:
Come      come close
She said like a god's
Wild mistress said come
On boy, I'm what you come

Out here in the bushes for. She burned alive
In her smell, and the eyes she looked at burned
With gratitude, thrown a point-eared scrap
Of the world's women, hot-tailed and hunted: she bit down
Hard on a great yell
To the house being eaten alive
By April's leaves. Bawled; they came and found.
The children cried

Helping tote to the full moon
Of the kitchen      "I carried the head"      O full of eyes
Heads kept coming across, and friends and family
Hurt      hurt
The spirit of the household, on the kitchen
Table being thick-sewed      they saying it was barbed
Wire looked like
It got him, and he had no business running

Off like that. Black lips curled as they bathed off
Blood, bathed blood. Staggered up under
The table making loud
A low-born sound, and went feeling

For the outer limits
Of the woods      felt them break and take in
The world      the frame turn loose and the house
Not mean what it said it was. Lay down and out
Of sight and could not get up
The head, lying on God's foot firesided
Fireheaded      formed a thought

Of Spring          of trees in wildfire
Of the mind speeded up          and put all thirst

Into the leaves. They grew
Unlimited. Soap boiled
Between black lips: the house
Spirit jumped up beyond          began to run          shot
Through the yard and bit down
On the youngest child. And when it sprang down
And out across the pasture, the grains of its footprints leapt
Free, where horses that shied from its low

New sound were gathered, and men swung themselves
Up to learn what Spring
Had a new way to tell, by bringing up
And out the speed of the fields. A long horn blew
Firesided          the mad head sang
Along the furrows          bouncing and echoing from earth
To earth through the body
Turning          doubling back
Through the weather of love running wild and the horses full

Of strangers coming after. Fence wire fell and rose
Flaming with messages as the spirit ran
Ran with house-hair
Burr-picking madly          and after came

Men          horses          spirits
Of households leaping crazily beyond
Their limits, dragging their bodies by the foaming throat through grass
And beggar-lice and by the red dust
Road where men blazed and roared
With their shoulders          blew it down and apart where it ran
And lay down on the earth of God's
One foot and the foot beneath the table kicked
The white mouth shut: this was something

In Spring in mild brown eyes          as strangers
Cut off the head and carried and held it
Up, blazing with consequence          blazing
With freedom saying          bringing
Help          help          madness          help.

# THE EYE-BEATERS

[for Mary Bookwalter]

*A man visits*
*a Home for chil-*
*dren in Indiana,*
*some of whom*
*have gone blind*
*there.*

Come something     come blood sunlight     come and they break
Through the child-wall, taking heart from the two left feet
Of your sound: are groping for the Visitor in the tall corn
Green of Indiana. You may be the light, for they have seen it
                                                    coming
From people: have seen it on cricket and brick have seen it
Seen it fade     seen slowly the edge of things fail     all corn
Green fail     heard fields grind     press with insects and go round
To the back of the head. They are blind. Listen     listen well
To your walking that gathers the blind in bonds     gathers these

*A therapist*
*explains why*
*the children*
*strike*
*their eyes.*

Who have fought with themselves     have blacked their eyes wide
Open, toddling like dolls and like penguins     soft-knotted down,
Protected, arms bound to their sides in gauze, but dark is not
To be stood in that way: they holler     howl till they can shred
Their gentle ropes     whirl and come loose. They *know* they
                                                    should see
But *what*, now? When their fists smash their eyeballs, they behold
                                                    no
Stranger giving light from his palms. What they glimpse has flared
In mankind from the beginning. In the asylum, children turn to
                                                    go back
Into the race: turn their heads without comment into the black
                                                    magic
Migraine of caves. Smudge-eyed, wide-eyed, gouged, horned, caved-
in, they are silent: it is for you to guess what they hold back inside
The brown and hazel     inside the failed green     the vacant
                                                    blue-

*The Visitor*
*begins to*
*invent a*
*fiction to*
*save his mind.*

eyed floating of the soul. Was that lightning     was that a heart-
struck leap     somewhere before birth? Why do you eat the green
                                                    summer
Air like smoky meat? Ah, Stranger, you do not visit this place,
You live or die in it     you brain-scream you beat your eyes to
                                                    see
The junebug take off backwards     spin     connect his body-sound

To what he is in the air. But under the fist, on the hand-stomped
                                                                bone,
A bison leaps out of rock     fades     a long-haired nine-year-old
                                                                clubs
Her eye, imploding with vision     dark     bright again     again
                                                                again
A beast, before her arms are tied. Can it be? Lord, when they slug
Their blue cheeks blacker, can it be that they do not see the wings
And green of insects     or the therapist suffering kindly     but
                                                a tribal light old

Enough to be seen without sight? There, quiet children stand
                                                                watching
A man striped and heavy with pigment, lift his hand with color
                                                                coming
From him. Bestial, working like God, he moves on stone he is
                                                                drawing
A half-cloud of beasts on the wall. They crane closer, helping,
                                                                beating
Harder, light blazing inward from their fists     and see     see
                                                                leap
From the shocked head-nerves, great herds of deer on the hacked
                                                                glory plain
Of the cave wall: antelope     elk: blind children strike for the
                                                                middle
Of the brain, where the race is young. Stranger, they stand here
And fill your mind with beasts: ibex     quagga     rhinoceros of
                                                                wool-
gathering smoke: cave bear     aurochs     mammoth: beings
                                                        that appear
Only in the memory of caves     the niches filled, not with
                                                        Virgins,
But with the squat shapes of the Mother. In glimmers of mid-
                                                        brain pain
The forms of animals are struck like water from the stone     where
                                                                hunger
And rage     where the Visitor's helplessness and terror     all
Move on the walls and create.
                    (Look up: the sun is taking its stand on four
        o'clock of Indiana time, painfully blazing     fist of a ball of fire
God struck from His one eye).
                    No; you see only dead beasts playing

In the bloody handprint on the stone where God gropes like a
                                                        man
Like a child, for animals      where the artist hunts and slashes,
                                                        glowing
Like entrail-blood, tracking the wounded game across the limestone
As it is conceived. The spoor leads      his hand changes      grows
Hair like a bison      horns like an elk      unshapes      in a deer-
                                                        leap emerges
From the spear-pitted rock, becoming what it can make
                                                        unrolling
Not sparing itself clenching re-forming rising      beating
For light.
                *Ah, you think it, Stranger: you'd like that you try hard*

His Reason
argues with his
invention.

*To think it, to think for them. But what you see, in the half-*
                                                        *inner sight*
*Of squinting, are only fields      only children whose hands are tied*
                                                        *away*
*From them for their own good      children waiting to smash*
                                                        *their dead*
*Eyes, live faces, to see nothing. As before, they come to you smiling,*
*Using their strange body-English. But why is it this they have*
                                                        *made up*
*In your mind? Why painting and Hunting? Why animals showing*
                                                        *how God*
*Is subject to the pictures in the cave      their clotted colors*
                                                        *like blood*
*On His hands as the wild horse burns      as the running buck*
                                                        *turns red*
*From His palm, while children twist in their white ropes, eyes*
                                                        *wide,*
*Their heads in the dark meat of bruises?*
                                        And now, blind hunters,
Swaying in concert like corn      sweet-faced      tribe-swaying at
                                                        the red wall
Of the blind like a cooking-fire      shoulder-moving, moaning as the
                                                        cave-
artist moaned when he drew the bull-elk to the heart      come
                                                        ring
Me round. I will undo you. Come, and your hands will be free to fly
Straight into your faces, and shake the human vision to its roots.
Flint-chipping sparks spring up: I can see      feel      see
                                                        another elk

Ignite with his own becoming: it is time.

Yes, indeed I know it is not

So      I am trying to make it      make something      make them

make me

Re-invent the vision of the race      knowing the blind must see

By magic or nothing. Therapists, I admit it; it helps me to think

That they can give themselves, like God from their scabby fists,

the original

Images of mankind: that when they beat their eyes, I witness

how

I survive, in my sun-blinded mind: that the beasts are calling to

God

And man for art, when the blind open wide and strike their incurable

eyes

In Indiana. *And yet, O Stranger, those beasts and mother-*

*figures are all*

*Made up by you. They are your therapy. There is nothing inside*

*their dark,*

*Nothing behind their eyes but the nerve that kills the sun above*

*the corn*

*Field      no hunt no meat no pain-struck spark no vision      no*

*pre-history*

*For the blind      nothing but blackness forever      nothing but*

*a new bruise*

*Risen upon the old.*

They have gone away; the doors have shut

shut on you

*The children retire, but he hears them behind their wall.*

And your makeshift salvation. Yet your head still keeps what you

would put in theirs

If you were God. Bring down your lids like a cave, and try to see

By the race alone. Collective memory stirs      herd-breathes

stamps

In snow-smoke, as the cave takes hold. You are artist and beast and

The picture of the beast: you are a ring of men and the

stampeded bones

Tumbling into the meat-pit. A child screams out in fury, but

where,

In the time of man? O brother, quiver and sweat: It is true that

no thing

Anyone can do is good enough for them: not Braille not data

Processing      not "learning TV repair" not music      no, and

not not being

(53)

"A burden": none of these, but only vision: what they see must
be crucial
*He accepts his fiction.*
To the human race. It is so; to let you live with yourself after seeing
Them, they must be thought to see by what has caused      is
causing us all
To survive. In the late sun of the asylum, you know nothing else
will do
You; the rest is mere light. In the palm of the hand the color red
is calling
For blood      the forest-fire roars on the cook-stone, smoke-
smothered and lightning-
born      and the race hangs on meat and illusion      hangs on
nothing
But a magical art. Stranger, you may as well take your own life
Blood      brain-blood, as vision. Yes; that hammering on the
door is not
Your heart, or the great pulse of insects; it is blind children
beating
Their eyes to throw a picture on the wall. Once more you hear
a child yell
In pure killing fury      pure triumph pure acceptance      as
his hands burst
Their bonds. It is happening. Half-broken light flickers with agony
Like a head      throwing up the beast-paint the wall cannot
shake
For a million years.
                    *Hold on to your fantasy; it is all that can save*
*A man with good eyes in this place. Hold on, though doctors*
*keep telling*
*You to back off      to be what you came as      back off from*
*the actual*
*Wall of their screaming room, as green comes all around you with*
*its ears*
*Of corn, its local, all-insect hum, given junebugs and flies*
*wherever*
*They are, in midair.* No;
                    by God. There is no help for this but madness,
Perversity. Think that somewhere under their pummeled lids
they gather
At the wall of art-crazed beasts, and the sun blazing into the
blackout
Of the cave, dies of vision. A spell sways in. It is time for the night

(54)

Hunt, and the wild meat of survival. The wall glimmers that God
                                                                    and man
Never forgot. I have put history out. An innocent eye, it is closed
Off, outside in the sun. Wind moans like an artist. The tribal
                                                    children lie
On their rocks in their animal skins    seeing in spurts of
                                                    eye-beating
Dream, the deer, still wet with creation, open its image to the heart's

*He leaves*
*the Home.*
Blood, as I step forward, as I move through the beast-paint of
                                                    the stone,
Taken over, submitting, brain-weeping. Light me a torch with
                                        what we have preserved
Of lightning. Cloud bellows in my hand. Good man hunter artist
                                                    father
Be with me. My prey is rock-trembling, calling. Beast, get in
My way. Your body opens onto the plain. Deer, take me into
                                                    your life-
lined form. I merge, I pass beyond in secret    in perversity and the
                                                    sheer
Despair of invention    my double-clear bifocals off    my
                                            reason gone
Like eyes. Therapist, farewell at the living end. Give me my spear.

# TURNING AWAY

*Variations on Estrangement*

## I

Something for a long time has gone wrong,
Got in between this you and that one other
And now      here      you must turn away.

Beyond! Beyond! Another life moves

In numbing clarity begins
By looking out the simple-minded window,
The face untimely relieved
Of living the expression of its love.

## II

Shy, sad, adolescent      separated-out
The gaze stands alone in the meadow
Like a king starting out on a journey
Away from all things that he knows.
It stands there      there

With the ghost's will to see and not tell
What it sees with its nerveless vision
Of sorrow, its queen-killing glare:
The apple tree in the wind
Paling with noon sleep,
Light pouring down from the day-moon
White-hot inside the sun's mildness,

The eyes clamped by an ordinary meadow
As by the latest masterpiece
Under the sun.

(56)

## III

For the face a studded look slowly
Arrives from a gulley of chickweed
Like a beard, come from something
Unwanted, that the face cannot help all its life.
Hair curls inside the jaws
Unstoppable    mindless    turns white
Turns straight    chokes
Helplessly, in more and more dangerous
Iron-masked silence.

## IV

A deadly, dramatic compression
Is made of the normal brow. Because of it
The presence of the hand upon the sill
Calms and does not shake the thing beheld.
Every stone within sight stands ready
To give you its secret
Of impassivity, its unquestionable
Silence: you wear
Its reason for existence where you stand

So still    the tongue grows solid also
Holding back the rock speech.

## V

A hooked shape threads
Through your nostrils, and you have
Caesar's eagle look, and nothing
For it to do,
Even though, on the golden
Imperial helmet, little doors close over
Your face, and your head is covered
With military flowers.

## VI

Turning away,
You foresee the same fields you watch.
They are there an instant
Before they are ready: a stream being slowly suspended
Between its weeds, running where it once was,
Keeping its choir-sounds going
All like crowned boys
But now among grasses that are
An enormous green bright growing No
That frees forever.


## VII

The mutual scar on the hand of man
And woman, earned in the kitchen,
Comes forth      rises for you to brush
Off like a cutworm
As the weed with wings explodes
In air, laying in front of you down
Cheap flowers by hundreds of thousands
And you try to get by heart
The words written after the end

Of every marriage manual, back
To the beginning, saying
Change; form again; flee.


## VIII

Despair and exultation
Lie down together and thrash
In the hot grass, no blade moving,
A stark freedom primes your new loins:
Turning away, you can breed
With the farthest women

And the farthest also in time: breed
Through bees, like flowers and bushes:

Breed Greeks, Egyptians and Romans     hoplites
Peasants     caged kings     clairvoyant bastards:
    The earth's whole history blazes
      To become this light
    For you are released to all others,

    All places and times of all women,
      And for their children hunger
    Also: for those who could be half
      You, half someone unmet,
Someone dead, immortal, or coming.

    Near you, some being suddenly
Also free, is weeping her body away.


## IX

    The watched fields shake     shake
      Half blind with scrutiny.
All working together, grasshoppers
      Push on a stem apiece
And the breathless meadow begins
    To sway     dissolve     revolve:

    Faintness     but the brain rights
      Itself with a sigh in the skull
      And sees again nothing
But intensified grass. Listen:
When this much is wrong, one can fix one's head

    In peacetime     turning away
    From an old peaceful love
    To a helmet of silent war
Against the universe     and see
What to do with it all: see with the eyes
    Of a very great general
      Roads ditches trees
Which have sunk their roots to provide
    Not shade but covering-fire.

## X

Somewhere in this guarded encampment
The soul stands stealthily up
To desert: stands up like the sex
About to run    running
Through pinewoods    creeks    changes of light    night
And day    the wide universe streaming over it
As it stands there panting    over-sensitized
Filled with blood from the feet

Heartbeating    surviving    in the last

Place    in cloud river meadowgrass or grave    waiting
For bird beast or plant to tell it
How to use itself    whom to meet    what to do
Which way to go to join
The most ineffectual army    the defiant, trembling
Corps of the unattached.

## XI

Fear passes
Into sweat hidden openly
In the instant new lines of the brow. The field
Deepens in peace, as though, even
Before battle, it were rich-
ening with a generation's
Thousand best, quietest men
In long grass bending east
To west. Turning away, seeing fearful
Ordinary ground, boys' eyes manlike go,
The middle-aged man's like a desperate
Boy's, the old man's like a new angel's

Beholding the river in all
White places    rushing
At and burning its boulders
Quietly    the current laid
In threads    as, idly, a conqueror's horse,

Ox-headed, is born of the shape of a cloud
That was an unnoticed
Deep-hanging bed.
Water waves in the air,
A slant, branded darkness
From a distant field full of horses
Uprisen into a cloud
That is their oversoul.


XII


Under the great drifting stallion
With his foreleg bloatedly cocked, the armed
Men who could spring from your teeth
Double their strength in your jaws:


XIII


So many battles
Fought in cow pastures     fought back
And forth over anybody's farm
With men or only
With wounded eyes—
Fought in the near yellow crops
And the same crops blue farther off.


XIV


Dead armies' breath like a sunflower
Stirs, where the loved-too-long
Lie with a whimper of scythes.
Coming to them, the seeds
Of distant plants either die
Or burn out when they touch
Ground, or are born in this place.
Rain is born rain: let tons of repossessed
Water walk to us!

## XV

You may have swallowed a thistle
Or the first drop of rain;
You have been open-mouthed.
Now speak of battles that bring

To light no blood, but strew the meadows
With inner lives:
Speak now with the thistle's sharpness
Piercing      floating      descending
In flowers all over the field
With a dog-noise low in the calyx.


## XVI

Like a hound, you can smell the earth change
As your cloud comes over the sun
Like a called horse.
The long field summons its armies
From every underground
Direction. Prepare to fight
The past      flee      lie down,
Heartbeat a noise in your head
Like knocking the rungs from a ladder:
So many things stand wide
Open! Distance is helplessly deep
On all sides      and you can enter, alone,
Anything      anything can go
On wherever it wishes   anywhere in the world or in time
But here and now.


## XVII

Turning away, the eyes do not mist over
Despite the alien sobbing in the room.
Withhold! Withhold! Stand by this window

As on guard
Duty     rehearsing what you will answer
If questioned     stand

General     deserter     freed slave belovèd of all,
Giving off behind your back
Ridiculous energy     stand

Like a proof of character learned
From Caesar's *Wars*     from novels
Read in the dark,
Thinking of your life as a thing
That can be learned,
As those earnest young heroes learned theirs,
Later, much later on.